PHILIPPIANS

Choosing Joy

LOVEGODGREATLY.COM

AT LOVE GOD GREATLY, YOU'LL FIND
REAL, AUTHENTIC WOMEN. WOMEN WHO
ARE IMPERFECT, YET FORGIVEN.

Women who desire less of us, and a whole lot
more of Jesus. Women who long to know God
through his Word, because we know that Truth
transforms and sets us free. Women who are
better together, saturated in God's Word and in
community with one another.

Welcome, friend. We're so glad you're here...

CONTENTS

WELCOME

We are glad you have decided to join us in this Bible study! First of all, please know that you have been prayed for! It is not a coincidence you are participating in this study.

Our prayer for you is simple: that you will grow closer to our Lord as you dig into His Word each and every day! As you develop the discipline of being in God's Word on a daily basis, our prayer is that you will fall in love with Him even more as you spend time reading from the Bible.

Each day before you read the assigned scripture(s), pray and ask God to help you understand it. Invite Him to speak to you through His Word. Then listen. It's His job to speak to you, and it's your job to listen and obey.

Take time to read the verses over and over again. We are told in Proverbs to search and you will find: "Search for it like silver, and hunt for it like hidden treasure. Then you will understand" (Prov. 2:4–5 NCV).

All of us here at Love God Greatly can't wait for you to get started, and we hope to see you at the finish line. Endure, persevere, press on—and don't give up! Finish well what you are beginning today. We will be here every step of the way, cheering you on! We are in this together. Fight to rise early, to push back the stress of the day, to sit alone and spend time in God's Word! Let's see what God has in store for you in this study! Journey with us as we learn to love God greatly with our lives!

As you go through this study, join us in the following resources below:

Weekly Blog Posts •

Weekly Memory Verses •

Weekly Monday Videos •

Weekly Challenges •

Facebook, Twitter, Instagram •

LoveGodGreatly.com •

Hashtags: #LoveGodGreatly •

RESOURCES

Join Us

ONLINE
lovegodgreatly.com

STORE
lovegodgreatly.com/store

FACEBOOK
facebook.com/LoveGodGreatly

INSTAGRAM
instagram.com/lovegodgreatlyofficial

TWITTER
@_LoveGodGreatly

DOWNLOAD THE APP

CONTACT US
info@lovegodgreatly.com

CONNECT
#LoveGodGreatly

LOVE
GOD
GREATLY

Love God Greatly (LGG) is a beautiful community of women who use a variety of technology platforms to keep each other accountable in God's Word. We start with a simple Bible reading plan, but it doesn't stop there.

Some women gather in homes and churches locally, while others connect online with women across the globe. Whatever the method, we lovingly lock arms and unite for this purpose: to love God greatly with our lives.

Would you consider reaching out and doing this study with someone?

In today's fast-paced technology-driven world, it would be easy to study God's Word in an isolated environment that lacks encouragement or support, but that isn't the intention here at Love God Greatly. God created us to live in community with Him and with those around us.

We need each other, and we live life better together. Because of this, would you consider reaching out and doing this study with someone?

Rest assured we'll be studying right alongside you—learning with you, cheering for you, enjoying sweet fellowship, and smiling from ear to ear as we watch God unite women together—intentionally connecting hearts and minds for His glory.

So here's the challenge: call your mom, your sister, your grandma, the girl across the street, or the college friend across the country. Gather a group of girls from your church or workplace, or meet in a coffee shop with friends you have always wished you knew better.

Arm-in-arm and hand-in-hand, let's do this thing...together.

SOAP STUDY
HOW AND WHY TO SOAP

In this study we offer you a study journal to accompany the verses we are reading. This journal is designed to help you interact with God's Word and learn to dig deeper, encouraging you to slow down and reflect on what God is saying to you that day.

At Love God Greatly, we use the SOAP Bible study method. Before beginning, let's take a moment to define this method and share why we recommend using it during your quiet time in the following pages.

It's one thing to simply read Scripture. But when you interact with it, intentionally slowing down to really reflect on it, suddenly words start popping off the page. The SOAP method allows you to dig deeper into Scripture and see more than you would if you simply read the verses and then went on your merry way.

The most important ingredients in the SOAP method are your interaction with God's Word and your application of His Word to your life:

Blessed is the one who does not walk in step with the wicked or stand in the way that sinners take or sit in the company of mockers, but whose delight is in the law of the LORD, and who meditates on his law day and night. That person is like a tree planted by streams of water, which yields its fruit in season and whose leaf does not wither—whatever they do prospers. (Ps. 1:1–3, NIV)

Please take the time to SOAP through our Bible studies and see for yourself how much more you get from your daily reading.

You'll be amazed.

The most important ingredients in the Soap method are your interaction with God's Word and your application of His Word to your life.

SOAP STUDY *(CONTINUED)*
WHAT DOES SOAP MEAN?

S STANDS FOR
SCRIPTURE

Physically write out the verses.

You'll be amazed at what God will reveal to you just by taking the time to slow down and write out what you are reading!

O STANDS FOR
OBSERVATION

What do you see in the verses that you're reading?

Who is the intended audience? Is there a repetition of words?

What words stand out to you?

MONDAY

READ
Colossians 1:5–8

SOAP
Colossians 1:5–8

Scripture

WRITE
OUT THE
SCRIPTURE
PASSAGE
FOR THE
DAY

The faith and love that spring from the hope stored up for you in heaven and about which you have already heard in the true message of the gospel that has come to you. In the same way, the gospel is bearing fruit and growing throughout the whole world just as it has been doing among you since the day you heard it and truly understood God's grace. You learned it from Epaphras our dear fellow servant, who is a faithful minister of Christ on our behalf, and who also told us of your love in the Spirit.

Observations

WRITE
DOWN 1 OR 2
OBSERVATIONS
FROM THE
PASSAGE.

When you combine faith and love, you get hope. We must remember that our hope is in heaven; it is yet to come. The gospel is the Word of truth. The gospel is continually bearing fruit and growing from the first day to the last. It just takes one person to change a whole community. Epaphras.

A STANDS FOR APPLICATION

This is when God's Word becomes personal.

What is God saying to you today?

How can you apply what you just read to your own personal life?

What changes do you need to make? Is there action you need to take?

Applications

WRITE DOWN 1 OR 2 APPLICATIONS FROM THE PASSAGE.

God used one man, Epaphras, to change a whole town. I was reminded that we are simply called to tell others about Christ; it is God's job to spread the gospel, to grow it, and have it bear fruit. I felt today's verses were almost directly spoken to Love God Greatly women: The gospel is bearing fruit and growing throughout the whole world just as it has been doing among you since the day you heard it and truly understood God's grace.

Pray

WRITE OUT A PRAYER OVER WHAT YOU LEARNED FROM TODAY'S PASSAGE.

Dear Lord, please help me to be an Epaphras, to tell others about You and then leave the results in Your loving hands. Please help me to understand and apply personally what I have read today to my life, thereby becoming more and more like You each and every day. Help me to live a life that bears the fruit of faith and love, anchoring my hope in heaven, not here on earth. Help me to remember that the best is yet to come!

P STANDS FOR PRAYER

Pray God's Word back to Him. Spend time thanking Him.

If He has revealed something to you during this time in His Word, pray about it.

If He has revealed some sin that is in your life, confess. And remember, He loves you dearly.

A RECIPE FOR YOU

PÖRKÖLT – HUNGARIAN MEAT STEW

Ingredients

3 pounds pork or beef

3 large onions, very finely minced

1 medium sweet tomato, chopped

3 yellow bell peppers, chopped

2 teaspoons salt (more to taste)

2 tablespoons sweet Hungarian paprika (more to taste)

3 tablespoons vegetable oil or lard

Directions

- In a large saute pan or pot, heat oil or lard over medium heat.
- Add minced onions and saute on medium heat, stirring frequently, for about 15 minutes. Do not let the onions get burned.
- While the onions are sautéing, cut the meat into 1 inch cubes (or smaller).
- Increase heat and add meat cubes to onion pan, stirring and searing the meat for 3-5 minutes.
- Decrease heat to medium low and add a bit of water if needed, just enough to barely cover the meat.
- Add salt, paprika, bell peppers, and tomatoes.
- Loosely cover the pot and simmer on low for about 1 hour 30 min. Add more water and stir as needed.
- Serve Pörkölt over Nokedli (Hungarian dumplings, see below), over rice or egg pasta.

NOKEDLI

Ingredients

approximately 1 gallon of water for cooking

2 teaspoons salt

1 tablespoon vegetable oil

2 cups all-purpose flour

1 teaspoon salt

4 large room-temperature eggs

Water (approximately 3/4 to 1 cup)

Directions

- Put a large saucepan of water on to boil. Add 2 teaspoons salt and oil to the water.
- In a large bowl, whisk together flour and 1 teaspoon salt. With a wooden spoon, stir in eggs and just enough water (anywhere from 3/4 to 1 cup) to make a wet, pourable dough. Don't beat it smooth. It should look like cottage cheese.
- Let the dough rest while the water comes to a boil. The dough should be cooked in three batches.
- Use a spaetzle plane (or cut the dough into small pieces using a spoon) and form dumplings to add to the boiling water.
- Repeat until you have used all the dough. Stir the nokedli so they don't stick to the bottom of the pot.
- After the nokedli rise to the surface, cook an additional minute or so. Taste one for doneness. Using a sieve or slotted spoon, transfer the cooked nokedli to a bowl with a little vegetable oil at the bottom. Stir to coat the dumplings so they don't stick together.
- Serve in soup or with stew. Leftovers can be refrigerated or frozen with good result.

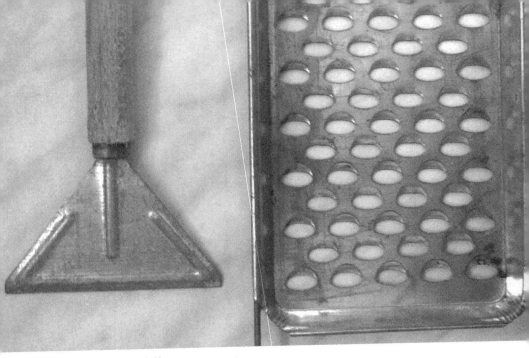

Traditional Hungarian Spaetzle Plane

CUCUMBER SALAD

Ingredients

2 large and long cucumbers, peeled

2 cloves garlic

2 tablespoons white vinegar

2 tablespoons granulated sugar

2 teaspoons salt

Sour cream for garnish

Hungarian paprika and black pepper for garnish

Directions

- Begin by slicing the cucumbers on a mandoline set to 1/8" thickness. Note: While a mandoline is best for ensuring paper thin slices, you can also just use a knife, making sure to slice the cucumber as thin as possible.

- Add the cucumbers to a large bowl with the salt and let it sit for half an hour.

- Add the minced garlic, white vinegar, and sugar. It should have a strong sweet-sour taste to make the cucumbers tasty. Stir to combine ingredients.

- Cover the bowl and refrigerate, stirring occasionally, for at least one hour prior to serving.

- When ready to serve, use a slotted spoon to transfer the salad into serving dishes.

- Top with some sour cream, ground black pepper and a dash of Hungarian paprika.

LGG HUNGARIAN TESTIMONY

JOLIKA, SLOVAKIA

My name is Jolika Nagy Rontóné. I am 57 years old and live in Slovakia. Slovakia used to be part of Hungary until the First World War. Hungarians now live here as a minority group and have to fight to keep their language and national identity.

A few years ago - when my kids were already grown and gone from the home - I was struggling in my broken marriage and felt terribly lonely and abandoned. My kids wanted to help me so they set up a Facebook account for me to find friends and entertainment. I was flooded with information that seemed useless, and for a long time I saw no point in using the site and thought that it was a foolish way to spend my time.

Every word I read was like a healing balm to my soul.

One day, however, my life took a huge turn. One of my dear friends invited me to participate in a Love God Greatly Bible study on Facebook. I accepted the invitation because I felt a deep desire to belong to a community of believers. I live in a tiny village and attend a very small church, so I have little opportunity throughout the week for local fellowship and Bible study. My first LGG study was in December during the Advent season. You have no idea how much this first study helped me to grow spiritually! Every word I read was like a healing balm to my soul. I was amazed that even though our group members came from so many different walks of life and had never met each other in person before, there was still such love and deep understanding among the women. In fact, I was so moved by the testimonies and SOAP comments of others that I felt that they could have been written by me!

I continued to quietly study with my group, soaking in the Word and enjoying the fellowship. I was so blessed by the encouragement from my group facilitator Viola Bolbás, and it wasn't until the end of my third Bible study that I dared to write a shy little thank you note and tried to excuse myself for being a quiet member. From this point on, things sped up and I started to write more and more comments. Today I am part of the ministry team, working with those who help make the studies happen. My Bible study group is a huge blessing for me. I have never missed a study since I joined LGG, and I feel that these studies have become an essential part of my life. Every study prompts me to self-examination, and I have changed so much for the better. I always marvel that we study topics I need to learn about and grow in the most!

It is because of LGG that I now study the Word of God on a daily basis. I no longer blame others for my misery. Instead, I am working on sweeping out all of the trash from my soul and I am digging deeply to find the person God sees in me. My circumstances haven't changed much, but I have real peace and joy in my Lord Jesus Christ. My LGG group is like a second family to me!

I would like more and more women to join Love God Greatly studies because I am convinced that when we are walking closely with God, He can use us as useful tools in spreading the gospel. I am so thankful to belong to LGG. I am also grateful for Facebook, as it gives us an opportunity to be in unity with others near and far, and we can use it to reach many women who have never heard the gospel before. Glory and thanks be to God for all this!

***To connect with
LGG Hungarian Branch:***

- szeresdnagyonistent.hu
- facebook.com/Szeresd-
  Nagyon-Istent-LGG-
  Hungary-131310280372910
- lgghungary@gmail.com

Do you know someone who
could use our Love God Greatly
Bible studies in Hungarian? If so,
make sure and tell them about
LGG Hungarian and all the
amazing Bible study resources we
provide to help equip them with
God's Word!!!

PHILIPPIANS

Choosing Joy

Let's Begin

INTRODUCTION

PHILIPPIANS

Welcome to our study of the book of Philippians. Philippians is actually a letter written to the Christians in Philippi, a place that Paul visited on his second missionary journey. Interestingly, it was named after Philip of Macedonia, the father of Alexander the Great.

This letter has a very informal tone, giving the impression that Paul was close to the people there. It is clear these believers have a special place in his heart.

Philippians is a favorite book for many because of its emphasis on joy, mixed with an uplifting and encouraging tone. This is pretty amazing considering it was written by Paul while he was in prison. These four chapters show us that the power of the Lord has the ability to make us rise above our circumstances and experience joy, contentment, and love for others. Speaking of joy, did you ever sing the song, "I've got the joy, joy, joy, joy down in my heart…"? It's a children's Sunday school song, and whenever I read Philippians this song pops into my head.

Joy is a dominant theme in this letter. Since Paul mentions it about 17 times, it is something that deserves our great attention. How is it possible to have deep joy in the midst of overwhelming sorrow and suffering? Paul is not only a great example to us, but he also points us to the answer. Philippians has 104 verses and Jesus is mentioned directly or indirectly 51 times. That says a lot about what the ultimate theme of this book is. In the end Paul will teach us that greater than joy is Jesus: the Author of our joy.

Without Jesus there is no salvation, and therefore no lasting joy. Without Jesus there is no way to overcome our circumstances, to love people who are hard to love, to reconcile, to forgive, and to live godly lives.

Augustine said, "Where your pleasure is, there is your treasure; Where your treasure is, there is your heart; Where your heart is, there is your happiness."

Let's open our Bibles and seek to better know our Savior and the joy he offers to those who follow him.

"These things I have spoken to you, that my joy may be in you, and that your joy may be full."

John 15:11

READING PLAN

WEEK 1
Joy in suffering

Monday
READ: PHILIPPIANS 1:1-6 • SOAP: 1:6

Tuesday
READ: PHILIPPIANS 1:7-11 • SOAP: 1:9-11

Wednesday
READ: PHILIPPIANS 1:12-14 • SOAP: 1:14

Thursday
READ: PHILIPPIANS 1:15-18 • SOAP: 1:18

Friday
READ: PHILIPPIANS 1:19-30 • SOAP: 1:21, 27

WEEK 2
Joy in serving

Monday
READ: PHILIPPIANS 2:1-4 • SOAP: 2:3-4

Tuesday
READ: PHILIPPIANS 2:5-11 • SOAP: 2:9-11

Wednesday
READ: PHILIPPIANS 2:12-13 • SOAP: 2:13

Thursday
READ: PHILIPPIANS 2:14-18 • SOAP: 2:14-16

Friday
READ: PHILIPPIANS 2:19-30 • SOAP: 2:20-21

WEEK 3
Joy in believing

Monday
READ: PHILIPPIANS 3:1-4 • SOAP: 3:3

Tuesday
READ: PHILIPPIANS 3:5-11 • SOAP: 3:8-9

Wednesday
READ: PHILIPPIANS 3:12-14 • SOAP: 3:12-14

Thursday
READ: PHILIPPIANS 3:15-19 • SOAP: 3:16

Friday
READ: PHILIPPIANS 3:20-21 • SOAP: 3:20

READING PLAN *(CONTINUED)*

WEEK 4
Joy in giving

Monday
READ: PHILIPPIANS 4:1-5 • SOAP: 4:4-5

Tuesday
READ: PHILIPPIANS 4:6-7 • SOAP: 4:6-7

Wednesday
READ: PHILIPPIANS 4:8-9 • SOAP: 4:8

Thursday
READ: PHILIPPIANS 4:10-13 • SOAP: 4:12-13

Friday
READ: PHILIPPIANS 4:14-23 • SOAP: 4:19

YOUR GOALS

We believe it's important to write out goals for this study. Take some time now and write three goals you would like to focus on as you begin to rise each day and dig into God's Word. Make sure and refer back to these goals throughout the next four weeks to help you stay focused. You can do it!

1.

2.

3.

Signature:

Date:

WEEK 1

Joy in suffering

And it is my prayer that your love may abound more and more, with knowledge and all discernment, so that you may approve what is excellent, and so be pure and blameless for the day of Christ,

Philippians 1:9-10

PRAYER

Prayer focus for this week:
Spend time praying for your family members.

MONDAY

TUESDAY

WEDNESDAY

THURSDAY

FRIDAY

CHALLENGE

You can find this listed in our Monday blog post.

MONDAY
Scripture for Week 1

Philippians 1:1-6

1 Paul and Timothy, servants of Christ Jesus,

To all the saints in Christ Jesus who are at Philippi, with the overseers and deacons:

2 Grace to you and peace from God our Father and the Lord Jesus Christ.

3 I thank my God in all my remembrance of you, 4 always in every prayer of mine for you all making my prayer with joy, 5 because of your partnership in the gospel from the first day until now. 6 And I am sure of this, that he who began a good work in you will bring it to completion at the day of Jesus Christ.

MONDAY

READ:
Philippians 1:1-6

SOAP:
Philippians 1:6

Scripture

WRITE
OUT THE
SCRIPTURE
PASSAGE
FOR THE
DAY.

Observations

WRITE
DOWN 1 OR 2
OBSERVATIONS
FROM THE
PASSAGE.

Applications

WRITE
DOWN 1 OR 2
APPLICATIONS
FROM THE
PASSAGE.

Pray

WRITE OUT
A PRAYER
OVER WHAT
YOU LEARNED
FROM TODAY'S
PASSAGE.

TUESDAY

Scripture for Week 1

Philippians 1:7-11

7 It is right for me to feel this way about you all, because
I hold you in my heart, for you are all partakers with me
of grace, both in my imprisonment and in the defense and
confirmation of the gospel. 8 For God is my witness, how
I yearn for you all with the affection of Christ Jesus. 9 And
it is my prayer that your love may abound more and
more, with knowledge and all discernment, 10 so that
you may approve what is excellent, and so be pure and
blameless for the day of Christ, 11 filled with the fruit of
righteousness that comes through Jesus Christ, to the glory
and praise of God.

TUESDAY

READ:
Philippians 1:7-11

SOAP:
Philippians 1:9-11

Scripture

WRITE
OUT THE
SCRIPTURE
PASSAGE
FOR THE
DAY.

Observations

WRITE
DOWN 1 OR 2
OBSERVATIONS
FROM THE
PASSAGE.

Applications

WRITE
DOWN 1 OR 2
APPLICATIONS
FROM THE
PASSAGE.

Pray

WRITE OUT
A PRAYER
OVER WHAT
YOU LEARNED
FROM TODAY'S
PASSAGE.

WEDNESDAY
Scripture for Week 1

Philippians 1:12-14

12 I want you to know, brothers, that what has happened to me has really served to advance the gospel, 13 so that it has become known throughout the whole imperial guard and to all the rest that my imprisonment is for Christ. 14 And most of the brothers, having become confident in the Lord by my imprisonment, are much more bold to speak the word without fear.

WEDNESDAY

READ:
Philippians 1:12-14

SOAP:
Philippians 1:14

Scripture

WRITE
OUT THE
SCRIPTURE
PASSAGE
FOR THE
DAY.

Observations

WRITE
DOWN 1 OR 2
OBSERVATIONS
FROM THE
PASSAGE.

Applications

WRITE DOWN 1 OR 2 APPLICATIONS FROM THE PASSAGE.

Pray

WRITE OUT A PRAYER OVER WHAT YOU LEARNED FROM TODAY'S PASSAGE.

THURSDAY
Scripture for Week 1

Philippians 1:15-18

15 Some indeed preach Christ from envy and rivalry,
but others from good will. 16 The latter do it out of
love, knowing that I am put here for the defense of the
gospel. 17 The former proclaim Christ out of selfish
ambition, not sincerely but thinking to afflict me in my
imprisonment. 18 What then? Only that in every way,
whether in pretense or in truth, Christ is proclaimed, and in
that I rejoice. Yes, and I will rejoice,

THURSDAY

READ:
Philippians 1:15-18

SOAP:
Philippians 1:18

Scripture

WRITE
OUT THE
SCRIPTURE
PASSAGE
FOR THE
DAY.

Observations

WRITE
DOWN 1 OR 2
OBSERVATIONS
FROM THE
PASSAGE.

Applications

WRITE
DOWN 1 OR 2
APPLICATIONS
FROM THE
PASSAGE.

Pray

WRITE OUT
A PRAYER
OVER WHAT
YOU LEARNED
FROM TODAY'S
PASSAGE.

FRIDAY

Scripture for Week 1

Philippians 1:19-30

19 for I know that through your prayers and the help of the Spirit of Jesus Christ this will turn out for my deliverance, 20 as it is my eager expectation and hope that I will not be at all ashamed, but that with full courage now as always Christ will be honored in my body, whether by life or by death.21 For to me to live is Christ, and to die is gain. 22 If I am to live in the flesh, that means fruitful labor for me. Yet which I shall choose I cannot tell. 23 I am hard pressed between the two. My desire is to depart and be with Christ, for that is far better. 24 But to remain in the flesh is more necessary on your account.25 Convinced of this, I know that I will remain and continue with you all, for your progress and joy in the faith, 26 so that in me you may have ample cause to glory in Christ Jesus, because of my coming to you again.

27 Only let your manner of life be worthy of the gospel of Christ, so that whether I come and see you or am absent, I may hear of you that you are standing firm in one spirit, with one mind striving side by side for the faith of the gospel, 28 and not frightened in anything by your opponents. This is a clear sign to them of their destruction, but of your salvation, and that from God. 29 For it has been granted to you that for the sake of Christ you should not only believe in him but also suffer for his sake, 30 engaged in the same conflict that you saw I had and now hear that I still have.

FRIDAY

READ:
Philippians 1:19-30

SOAP:
Philippians 1:21, 27

Scripture

WRITE
OUT THE
SCRIPTURE
PASSAGE
FOR THE
DAY.

Observations

WRITE
DOWN 1 OR 2
OBSERVATIONS
FROM THE
PASSAGE.

Applications

WRITE
DOWN 1 OR 2
APPLICATIONS
FROM THE
PASSAGE.

Pray

WRITE OUT
A PRAYER
OVER WHAT
YOU LEARNED
FROM TODAY'S
PASSAGE.

REFLECTION QUESTIONS

1. Verse 6 says that Jesus will bring the good work in us to completion. What does this mean?

2. Why is it important to couple love with knowledge and discernment (vs. 9)?

3. How did God turn Paul's imprisonment and sufferings to advantage?

4. What advantage is Paul referring to when he says, "to live is Christ"? What advantages might Paul be thinking of when he says, "to die is gain"?

5. Paul talks about not being frightened by our opponents. What might we be frightened of and how do we stand firm with courage?

NOTES

WEEK 2

Joy in serving

Do nothing from selfish ambition or conceit, but in humility count others more significant than yourselves.

Philippians 2:3

PRAYER
WRITE DOWN YOUR PRAYER REQUESTS
AND PRAISES FOR EACH DAY.

Prayer focus for this week:
Spend time praying for your country.

MONDAY

TUESDAY

WEDNESDAY

THURSDAY

FRIDAY

CHALLENGE
You can find this listed in our Monday blog post.

MONDAY
Scripture for Week 2

Philippians 2:1-4

1 So if there is any encouragement in Christ, any comfort
from love, any participation in the Spirit, any affection
and sympathy, 2 complete my joy by being of the same
mind, having the same love, being in full accord and of
one mind. 3 Do nothing from selfish ambition or conceit,
but in humility count others more significant than
yourselves. 4 Let each of you look not only to his own
interests, but also to the interests of others.

MONDAY

READ:
Philippians 2:1-4

SOAP:
Philippians 2:3-4

Scripture

WRITE
OUT THE
SCRIPTURE
PASSAGE
FOR THE
DAY.

Observations

WRITE
DOWN 1 OR 2
OBSERVATIONS
FROM THE
PASSAGE.

Applications

WRITE
DOWN 1 OR 2
APPLICATIONS
FROM THE
PASSAGE.

Pray

WRITE OUT
A PRAYER
OVER WHAT
YOU LEARNED
FROM TODAY'S
PASSAGE.

TUESDAY
Scripture for Week 2

Philippians 2:5-11

5 Have this mind among yourselves, which is yours
in Christ Jesus, 6 who, though he was in the form of
God, did not count equality with God a thing to be
grasped, 7 but emptied himself, by taking the form of
a servant, being born in the likeness of men. 8 And being
found in human form, he humbled himself by becoming
obedient to the point of death, even death on a
cross. 9 Therefore God has highly exalted him and bestowed
on him the name that is above every name, 10 so that at the
name of Jesus every knee should bow, in heaven and on earth
and under the earth, 11 and every tongue confess that Jesus
Christ is Lord, to the glory of God the Father.

TUESDAY

READ:
Philippians 2:5-11

SOAP:
Philippians 2:9-11

Scripture

WRITE
OUT THE
SCRIPTURE
PASSAGE
FOR THE
DAY.

Observations

WRITE
DOWN 1 OR 2
OBSERVATIONS
FROM THE
PASSAGE.

Applications

WRITE
DOWN 1 OR 2
APPLICATIONS
FROM THE
PASSAGE.

Pray

WRITE OUT
A PRAYER
OVER WHAT
YOU LEARNED
FROM TODAY'S
PASSAGE.

WEDNESDAY
Scripture for Week 2

Philippians 2:12-13

12 Therefore, my beloved, as you have always obeyed,
so now, not only as in my presence but much more in
my absence, work out your own salvation with fear and
trembling, 13 for it is God who works in you, both to will
and to work for his good pleasure.

WEDNESDAY

READ:
Philippians 2:12-13

SOAP:
Philippians 2:13

Scripture

WRITE
OUT THE
SCRIPTURE
PASSAGE
FOR THE
DAY.

Observations

WRITE
DOWN 1 OR 2
OBSERVATIONS
FROM THE
PASSAGE.

Applications

WRITE
DOWN 1 OR 2
APPLICATIONS
FROM THE
PASSAGE.

Pray

WRITE OUT
A PRAYER
OVER WHAT
YOU LEARNED
FROM TODAY'S
PASSAGE.

THURSDAY
Scripture for Week 2

Philippians 2:14-18

14 Do all things without grumbling or disputing, 15 that
you may be blameless and innocent, children of
God without blemish in the midst of a crooked and
twisted generation, among whom you shine as lights in the
world, 16 holding fast to the word of life, so that in the day
of Christ I may be proud that I did not run in vain or labor
in vain. 17 Even if I am to be poured out as a drink offering
upon the sacrificial offering of your faith, I am glad and
rejoice with you all. 18 Likewise you also should be glad and
rejoice with me.

THURSDAY

READ:
Philippians 2:14-18

SOAP:
Philippians 2:14-16

Scripture

WRITE
OUT THE
SCRIPTURE
PASSAGE
FOR THE
DAY.

Observations

WRITE
DOWN 1 OR 2
OBSERVATIONS
FROM THE
PASSAGE.

Applications

WRITE
DOWN 1 OR 2
APPLICATIONS
FROM THE
PASSAGE.

Pray

WRITE OUT
A PRAYER
OVER WHAT
YOU LEARNED
FROM TODAY'S
PASSAGE.

FRIDAY
Scripture for Week 2

Philippians 2:19-30

19 I hope in the Lord Jesus to send Timothy to you soon,
so that I too may be cheered by news of you. 20 For I have
no one like him, who will be genuinely concerned for your
welfare. 21 For they all seek their own interests, not those
of Jesus Christ. 22 But you know Timothy's proven worth,
how as a son with a father he has served with me in the
gospel. 23 I hope therefore to send him just as soon as I
see how it will go with me, 24 and I trust in the Lord that
shortly I myself will come also.

25 I have thought it necessary to send to you Epaphroditus
my brother and fellow worker and fellow soldier, and your
messenger and minister to my need, 26 for he has been
longing for you all and has been distressed because you heard
that he was ill. 27 Indeed he was ill, near to death. But God
had mercy on him, and not only on him but on me also, lest
I should have sorrow upon sorrow. 28 I am the more eager
to send him, therefore, that you may rejoice at seeing him
again, and that I may be less anxious. 29 So receive him in
the Lord with all joy, and honor such men, 30 for he nearly
died for the work of Christ, risking his life to complete what
was lacking in your service to me.

FRIDAY

READ:
Philippians 2:19-30

SOAP:
Philippians 2:20-21

Scripture

WRITE
OUT THE
SCRIPTURE
PASSAGE
FOR THE
DAY.

Observations

WRITE
DOWN 1 OR 2
OBSERVATIONS
FROM THE
PASSAGE.

Applications

WRITE
DOWN 1 OR 2
APPLICATIONS
FROM THE
PASSAGE.

Pray

WRITE OUT
A PRAYER
OVER WHAT
YOU LEARNED
FROM TODAY'S
PASSAGE.

REFLECTION QUESTIONS

1. List all of the godly character qualities found in Chapter 2. Which ones do you struggle with and why?

2. Why is obedience important?

3. We run the race by "holding fast to the word of life" (vs 16). What is the word of life and how do we hold on to it?

4. What is a drink offering and why was Paul willing to be poured out like one?

5. Paul was a real person with real feelings. How does this come through when he talks about Timothy and Epaphroditus?

NOTES

WEEK 3

Joy in believing

Indeed, I count everything as loss because of the surpassing worth of knowing Christ Jesus my Lord. For his sake I have suffered the loss of all things and count them as rubbish, in order that I may gain Christ

Philippians 3:8

PRAYER

Prayer focus for this week:
Spend time praying for your friends.

MONDAY

TUESDAY

WEDNESDAY

THURSDAY

FRIDAY

CHALLENGE

You can find this listed in our Monday blog post.

MONDAY

Scripture for Week 3

Philippians 3:1-4

1 Finally, my brothers, rejoice in the Lord. To write the same things to you is no trouble to me and is safe for you.

2 Look out for the dogs, look out for the evildoers, look out for those who mutilate the flesh. 3 For we are the circumcision, who worship by the Spirit of God and glory in Christ Jesus and put no confidence in the flesh— 4 though I myself have reason for confidence in the flesh also. If anyone else thinks he has reason for confidence in the flesh, I have more:

MONDAY

READ:
Philippians 3:1-4

SOAP:
Philippians 3:3

Scripture

WRITE
OUT THE
SCRIPTURE
PASSAGE
FOR THE
DAY.

Observations

WRITE
DOWN 1 OR 2
OBSERVATIONS
FROM THE
PASSAGE.

Applications

WRITE
DOWN 1 OR 2
APPLICATIONS
FROM THE
PASSAGE.

Pray

WRITE OUT
A PRAYER
OVER WHAT
YOU LEARNED
FROM TODAY'S
PASSAGE.

TUESDAY

Scripture for Week 3

Philippians 3:5-11

5 circumcised on the eighth day, of the people of Israel, of the tribe of Benjamin, a Hebrew of Hebrews; as to the law, a Pharisee; 6 as to zeal, a persecutor of the church; as to righteousness under the law, blameless. 7 But whatever gain I had, I counted as loss for the sake of Christ. 8 Indeed, I count everything as loss because of the surpassing worth of knowing Christ Jesus my Lord. For his sake I have suffered the loss of all things and count them as rubbish, in order that I may gain Christ 9 and be found in him, not having a righteousness of my own that comes from the law, but that which comes through faith in Christ, the righteousness from God that depends on faith— 10 that I may know him and the power of his resurrection, and may share his sufferings, becoming like him in his death, 11 that by any means possible I may attain the resurrection from the dead.

TUESDAY

READ:
Philippians 3:5-11

SOAP:
Philippians 3:8-9

Scripture

WRITE
OUT THE
SCRIPTURE
PASSAGE
FOR THE
DAY.

Observations

WRITE
DOWN 1 OR 2
OBSERVATIONS
FROM THE
PASSAGE.

Applications

WRITE
DOWN 1 OR 2
APPLICATIONS
FROM THE
PASSAGE.

Pray

WRITE OUT
A PRAYER
OVER WHAT
YOU LEARNED
FROM TODAY'S
PASSAGE.

WEDNESDAY
Scripture for Week 3

Philippians 3:12-14

12 Not that I have already obtained this or am already perfect, but I press on to make it my own, because Christ Jesus has made me his own. 13 Brothers, I do not consider that I have made it my own. But one thing I do: forgetting what lies behind and straining forward to what lies ahead, 14 I press on toward the goal for the prize of the upward call of God in Christ Jesus.

WEDNESDAY

READ:
Philippians 3:12-14

SOAP:
Philippians 3:12-14

Scripture

WRITE
OUT THE
SCRIPTURE
PASSAGE
FOR THE
DAY.

Observations

WRITE
DOWN 1 OR 2
OBSERVATIONS
FROM THE
PASSAGE.

Applications

WRITE
DOWN 1 OR 2
APPLICATIONS
FROM THE
PASSAGE.

Pray

WRITE OUT
A PRAYER
OVER WHAT
YOU LEARNED
FROM TODAY'S
PASSAGE.

THURSDAY
Scripture for Week 3

Philippians 3:15-19

15 Let those of us who are mature think this way, and if in anything you think otherwise, God will reveal that also to you. 16 Only let us hold true to what we have attained.

17 Brothers, join in imitating me, and keep your eyes on those who walk according to the example you have in us. 18 For many, of whom I have often told you and now tell you even with tears, walk as enemies of the cross of Christ. 19 Their end is destruction, their god is their belly, and they glory in their shame, with minds set on earthly things.

THURSDAY

READ:
Philippians 3:15-19

SOAP:
Philippians 3:16

Scripture

WRITE
OUT THE
SCRIPTURE
PASSAGE
FOR THE
DAY.

Observations

WRITE
DOWN 1 OR 2
OBSERVATIONS
FROM THE
PASSAGE.

Applications

WRITE
DOWN 1 OR 2
APPLICATIONS
FROM THE
PASSAGE.

Pray

WRITE OUT
A PRAYER
OVER WHAT
YOU LEARNED
FROM TODAY'S
PASSAGE.

FRIDAY
Scripture for Week 3

Philippians 3:20-21

20 But our citizenship is in heaven, and from it we await a Savior, the Lord Jesus Christ, 21 who will transform our lowly body to be like his glorious body, by the power that enables him even to subject all things to himself.

FRIDAY

READ:
Philippians 3:20-21

SOAP:
Philippians 3:20

Scripture

WRITE
OUT THE
SCRIPTURE
PASSAGE
FOR THE
DAY.

Observations

WRITE
DOWN 1 OR 2
OBSERVATIONS
FROM THE
PASSAGE.

Applications

WRITE
DOWN 1 OR 2
APPLICATIONS
FROM THE
PASSAGE.

Pray

WRITE OUT
A PRAYER
OVER WHAT
YOU LEARNED
FROM TODAY'S
PASSAGE.

REFLECTION QUESTIONS

1. What does it mean to rejoice in the Lord? Why is this important?

2. What is the danger of having "confidence in the flesh"?

3. Paul says that he is willing to count everything as loss compared to knowing Christ. How can we have this kind of mindset today?

4. What goal are we to press forward towards?

5. Explain what it means to have our citizenship in heaven. How should this impact the way we live? How should this impact what we teach the next generation?

NOTES

WEEK 4

Joy in giving

Finally, brothers, whatever is true, whatever is honorable, whatever is just, whatever is pure, whatever is lovely, whatever is commendable, if there is any excellence, if there is anything worthy of praise, think about these things.

Philippians 4:8

PRAYER

Prayer focus for this week:
Spend time praying for your church.

MONDAY

TUESDAY

WEDNESDAY

THURSDAY

FRIDAY

CHALLENGE

You can find this listed in our Monday blog post.

MONDAY
Scripture for Week 4

Philippians 4:1-5

1 Therefore, my brothers, whom I love and long for, my joy and crown, stand firm thus in the Lord, my beloved.

2 I entreat Euodia and I entreat Syntyche to agree in the Lord. 3 Yes, I ask you also, true companion, help these women, who have labored side by side with me in the gospel together with Clement and the rest of my fellow workers, whose names are in the book of life.

4 Rejoice in the Lord always; again I will say, rejoice. 5 Let your reasonableness be known to everyone. The Lord is at hand;

MONDAY

READ:
Philippians 4:1-5

SOAP:
Philippians 4:4-5

Scripture

WRITE
OUT THE
SCRIPTURE
PASSAGE
FOR THE
DAY.

Observations

WRITE
DOWN 1 OR 2
OBSERVATIONS
FROM THE
PASSAGE.

Applications

WRITE
DOWN 1 OR 2
APPLICATIONS
FROM THE
PASSAGE.

Pray

WRITE OUT
A PRAYER
OVER WHAT
YOU LEARNED
FROM TODAY'S
PASSAGE.

TUESDAY

Scripture for Week 4

Philippians 4:6-7

6 do not be anxious about anything, but in everything by prayer and supplication with thanksgiving let your requests be made known to God. 7 And the peace of God, which surpasses all understanding, will guard your hearts and your minds in Christ Jesus.

TUESDAY

READ:
Philippians 4:6-7

SOAP:
Philippians 4:6-7

Scripture

WRITE
OUT THE
SCRIPTURE
PASSAGE
FOR THE
DAY.

Observations

WRITE
DOWN 1 OR 2
OBSERVATIONS
FROM THE
PASSAGE.

Applications

WRITE
DOWN 1 OR 2
APPLICATIONS
FROM THE
PASSAGE.

Pray

WRITE OUT
A PRAYER
OVER WHAT
YOU LEARNED
FROM TODAY'S
PASSAGE.

WEDNESDAY

Scripture for Week 4

Philippians 4:8-9

8 Finally, brothers, whatever is true, whatever is honorable,
whatever is just, whatever is pure, whatever is lovely,
whatever is commendable, if there is any excellence, if
there is anything worthy of praise, think about these
things. 9 What you have learned and received and heard and
seen in me—practice these things, and the God of peace will
be with you.

WEDNESDAY

READ:
Philippians 4:8-9

SOAP:
Philippians 4:8

Scripture

WRITE
OUT THE
SCRIPTURE
PASSAGE
FOR THE
DAY.

Observations

WRITE
DOWN 1 OR 2
OBSERVATIONS
FROM THE
PASSAGE.

Applications

WRITE
DOWN 1 OR 2
APPLICATIONS
FROM THE
PASSAGE.

Pray

WRITE OUT
A PRAYER
OVER WHAT
YOU LEARNED
FROM TODAY'S
PASSAGE.

THURSDAY
Scripture for Week 4

Philippians 4:10-13
10 I rejoiced in the Lord greatly that now at length you have revived your concern for me. You were indeed concerned for me, but you had no opportunity. 11 Not that I am speaking of being in need, for I have learned in whatever situation I am to be content. 12 I know how to be brought low, and I know how to abound. In any and every circumstance, I have learned the secret of facing plenty and hunger, abundance and need. 13 I can do all things through him who strengthens me.

THURSDAY

READ:
Philippians 4:10-13

SOAP:
Philippians 4:12-13

Scripture

WRITE
OUT THE
SCRIPTURE
PASSAGE
FOR THE
DAY.

Observations

WRITE
DOWN 1 OR 2
OBSERVATIONS
FROM THE
PASSAGE.

Applications

WRITE
DOWN 1 OR 2
APPLICATIONS
FROM THE
PASSAGE.

Pray

WRITE OUT
A PRAYER
OVER WHAT
YOU LEARNED
FROM TODAY'S
PASSAGE.

FRIDAY
Scripture for Week 4

Philippians 4:14-23

14 Yet it was kind of you to share my trouble. 15 And you Philippians yourselves know that in the beginning of the gospel, when I left Macedonia, no church entered into partnership with me in giving and receiving, except you only. 16 Even in Thessalonica you sent me help for my needs once and again. 17 Not that I seek the gift, but I seek the fruit that increases to your credit. 18 I have received full payment, and more. I am well supplied, having received from Epaphroditus the gifts you sent, a fragrant offering, a sacrifice acceptable and pleasing to God. 19 And my God will supply every need of yours according to his riches in glory in Christ Jesus. 20 To our God and Father be glory forever and ever. Amen.

21 Greet every saint in Christ Jesus. The brothers who are with me greet you. 22 All the saints greet you, especially those of Caesar's household.

23 The grace of the Lord Jesus Christ be with your spirit.

FRIDAY

READ:
Philippians 4:14-23

SOAP:
Philippians 4:19

Scripture

WRITE
OUT THE
SCRIPTURE
PASSAGE
FOR THE
DAY.

Observations

WRITE
DOWN 1 OR 2
OBSERVATIONS
FROM THE
PASSAGE.

Applications

WRITE
DOWN 1 OR 2
APPLICATIONS
FROM THE
PASSAGE.

Pray

WRITE OUT
A PRAYER
OVER WHAT
YOU LEARNED
FROM TODAY'S
PASSAGE.

REFLECTION QUESTIONS

1. How can we become a person who is joyful in all circumstances?

2. How do we overcome anxiety and fear?

3. What are we to train our minds to think on?

4. What is contentment? How do we learn it?

5. As Christians we are called to bear one another's burdens and troubles. What does that require of us?

NOTES

KNOW THESE TRUTHS
from God's Word

God loves you.

Even when you're feeling unworthy and like the world is stacked against you, God loves you - yes, you - and He has created you for great purpose.

God's Word says, "God so loved the world that He gave His one and only Son, Jesus, that whoever believes in Him shall not perish, but have eternal life" (John 3:16).

Our sin separates us from God.

We are all sinners by nature and by choice, and because of this we are separated from God, who is holy.

God's Word says, "All have sinned and fall short of the glory of God" (Romans 3:23).

Jesus died so that you might have life.

The consequence of sin is death, but your story doesn't have to end there! God's free gift of salvation is available to us because Jesus took the penalty for our sin when He died on the cross.

God's Word says, "For the wages of sin is death, but the free gift of God is eternal life in Christ Jesus our Lord" (Romans 6:23); "God demonstrates His own love toward us, in that while we were yet sinners, Christ died for us" (Romans 5:8).

Jesus lives!

Death could not hold Him, and three days after His body was placed in the tomb Jesus rose again, defeating sin and death forever! He lives today in heaven and is preparing a place in eternity for all who believe in Him.

God's Word says, "In my Father's house are many rooms. If it were not so, would I have told you that I go to prepare a place for you? And if I go and prepare a place for you, I will come again and will take you to myself, that where I am you may be also" (John 14:2-3).

Yes, you can KNOW that you are forgiven.
Accept Jesus as the only way to salvation...

Accepting Jesus as your Savior is not about what you can do, but rather about having faith in what Jesus has already done. It takes recognizing that you are a sinner, believing that Jesus died for your sins, and asking for forgiveness by placing your full trust in Jesus's work on the cross on your behalf.

God's Word says, "If you confess with your mouth that Jesus is Lord and believe in your heart that God raised him from the dead, you will be saved. For with the heart one believes and is justified, and with the mouth one confesses and is saved" (Romans 10:9-10).

Practically, what does that look like?
With a sincere heart, you can pray a simple prayer like this:

God,
I know that I am a sinner.
I don't want to live another day without embracing
the love and forgiveness that You have for me.
I ask for Your forgiveness.
I believe that You died for my sins and rose from the dead.
I surrender all that I am and ask You to be Lord of my life.
Help me to turn from my sin and follow You.
Teach me what it means to walk in freedom as I live under Your grace,
and help me to grow in Your ways as I seek to know You more.
Amen.

If you just prayed this prayer (or something similar in your own words), would you email us at info@lovegodgreatly.com?

We'd love to help get you started on this exciting journey as a child of God!

WELCOME FRIEND

We're so glad you're here

Love God Greatly exists to inspire, encourage, and equip women all over the world to make God's Word a priority in their lives.

INSPIRE

women to make God's Word a priority in their daily lives through our Bible study resources.

ENCOURAGE

women in their daily walks with God through online community and personal accountability.

EQUIP

women to grow in their faith, so that they can effectively reach others for Christ.

Love God Greatly consists of a beautiful community of women who use a variety of technology platforms to keep each other accountable in God's Word.

We start with a simple Bible reading plan, but it doesn't stop there.

Some gather in homes and churches locally, while others connect online with women across the globe. Whatever the method, we lovingly lock arms and unite for this purpose...to Love God Greatly with our lives.

At Love God Greatly, you'll find real, authentic women. Women who are imperfect, yet forgiven. Women who desire less of us, and a whole lot more of Jesus. Women who long to know God through his Word, because we know that Truth transforms and sets us free. Women who are better together, saturated in God's Word and in community with one another.

Love God Greatly is a 501 (C) (3) non-profit organization. Funding for Love God Greatly comes through donations and proceeds from our online Bible study journals and books. LGG is committed to providing quality Bible study materials and believes finances should never get in the way of a woman being able to participate in one of our studies. All journals and translated journals are available to download for free from LoveGodGreatly.com for those who cannot afford to purchase them. Our journals and books are also available for sale on Amazon. Search for "Love God Greatly" to see all of our Bible study journals and books. 100% of proceeds go directly back into supporting Love God Greatly and helping us inspire, encourage and equip women all over the world with God's Word.

THANK YOU for partnering with us!

WHAT WE OFFER:

18 + Translations | Bible Reading Plans | Online Bible Study
Love God Greatly App | 80 + Countries Served
Bible Study Journals & Books | Community Groups

EACH LGG STUDY INCLUDES:

Three Devotional Corresponding Blog Posts | Monday Blog Videos
Memory Verses | Weekly Challenge | Weekly Reading Plan
Reflection Questions And More!

OTHER LOVE GOD GREATLY STUDIES INCLUDE:

David | Ecclesiastes | Growing Through Prayer | Names Of God
Galatians | Psalm 119 | 1st & 2nd Peter | Made For Community | Esther
The Road To Christmas | The Source Of Gratitude | You Are Loved

Visit us online at
LOVEGODGREATLY.COM

Made in the USA
Lexington, KY
31 October 2017